I0438012

DISCOVERY
OF
AGGRESSION

An Essay

by
Stefan Tanevski

authorHOUSE®

AuthorHouse™
1663 Liberty Drive, Suite 200
Bloomington, IN 47403
www.authorhouse.com
Phone: 1-800-839-8640

First published by AuthorHouse 2/20/2008

ISBN: 978-1-4343-6082-3 (sc)

Printed in the United States of America
Bloomington, Indiana

This book is printed on acid-free paper.

I CANNOT UNDERSTAND ANYMORE, HOW
WE COULDN'T REALIZE THE UNIVERSALITY
OF THE NONEROTIC AGGRESSIONS AND
DESTRUCTIONS, AND HOW WE COULD LET
GO TO ADD ADDITIONALLY COORESPOND
IMPORTANCE TO IT IN INTERPRETATION OF
LIFE

Sigmund Freud

SUMMARY

The problem of aggression has divided the researchers into two main groups.

The first group claims that aggression is a natural characteristic and explain it as an atavistic return to pre-human origins, with certain instincts which instigates aggression.

The second group claim that man, basically, is not aggressive by nature. They explain the human aggression with economic and legal circumstances in which some are poor with no rights, and humiliated; and others are rich, powerful, privileged. Thus, this conflict-prone condition provokes aggression.

I start from a so far completely unknown basis: that there is a SUBCONSCIOUS CONFLICT BETWEEN LIFE AND DEATH WITHIN MAN HIMSELF, WHICH IN THE CONSCIOUS LIVING IS REFLECTED AS AGGRESSION.

TABLE OF CONTENTS

DISCOVERY OF GENESIS
OF AGGRESSION

Every day experience shows us that the causes of aggression are the destructive elements of man, like hatred, envy, vengefulness, selfishness. Dostoevsky was the first to comprehend that the destructive psychological elements gaiety, joy, happiness, are also causes of aggression. He says:

> "Generally, in every misfortune of the neighbour, there is something gay in the eyes that look on – who ever you are."[1]

I.e., whatever scientific, artistic, theological knowledge or ignorance you have; if you are clerk, politician, engineer, doctor, merchant, artist, general, blacksmith, ploughman, beggar or king, when you confront your neighbour's misfortune you'll feel hidden or visible gaiety, joy, happiness. Also we have the converse relation: generally, in every happiness of the neighbour, there's something sad in the eyes that look on – whoever you are. Let's see this action.

[1] F.M. Dostoevsky: "Devils" p.345, Moscow 1957

One of two inseparable friends is informing the other that because of some creation of his he is to be rewarded and the reward will be money. As proof, the rewarded is showing the other the jury's letter. He was expressing all this in puffed up tones and with pompous gesticulations, from which it can be easily seen, that he's not feeling like "himself" as he was before, but with superior status. Listening to this, the non-rewarded felt more and more envious, and when hatred joined his envy, he suddenly kept a distance from his friend, without explanation. All that which had made these friends inseparable suddenly disappeared, as though had never existed. The non-rewarded even avoided accidental meetings with the rewarded.

In this instance, we see gaiety in the rewarded and envy in the non-rewarded. The gaiety and the envy were not kindled by the reward itself, but by something, which made a difference between these friends within their society, than – social status. Now, one has higher status than the other, i.e., one is superior over the other. The fact that the news of the reward provoked dramatic emotions in the non-rewarded says that he felt this superiority threatened him: was aggressive, and the conflict between these friends became unavoidable.

When aggression is satisfied by gaiety, joy, happiness it is: PASSIVE AGGRESSION. And when aggression uses intrigue, perjury, outrage; aiming to make someone unhappy, weak or tired, it is ACTIVE AGGRESSION.

Now, we must ask ourselves whether superiority over one's neighbour produces gaiety in the superior and sorrow in the degraded – or it is something else? To answer this question we'll move on to the conflict between life and death within man himself.

CONFLICT BETWEEN LIFE AND DEATH WITHIN MAN HIMSELF

Monotonous, but it' very essential, truth that man is not created by himself, because his aspirations must conform with the universe which he is created by and which has determined his fate. In order to live man must eat, drink and sleep; but he doesn't eat and drink everything because there are substances which would kill him if he ate or drank them. As it's dangerous to eat or drink everything, is it dangerous to KNOW all about the universe and future death? We can be sure that, because of the great communication between man's intuition and the outer world, and between his intuition and his organism, man intuitively knows the universe and the last act of his own being – death. As the senses are selecting agents for food and drink, is there also an agent which selects what we can or should know? Something is said in psychology about this, for instance:

> "The way in which dreams endeavour
> to avoid definite expression or ignore

> the decisive point often surprises me. Freud confirmed that there is particular function of the psyche, which he named "censor". I think that the censor turns the pictures of the dream over, makes them unrecognizable or false for the consciousness which is dreaming, in order to suppress the real content of the dream. Hiding the critical point from the dreamer, the censor is protecting the dreamer from the attacks of inconvenient dream patterns".[2]

It's obvious that the censor's place is among the processes of life and death, and the censor's function is to hide, or disguise, from the conscious mind the deadly dangers of existence itself. Thus, if some pathological process or threat from society threatens death, the censor blocks this dream, which is an expression of reality, or perverts its shape so that its meaning is hardly felt, because, if it allows the dreamer to see the truth, he may fall into psychosis, depression or psychological trauma. This means, that all happenings within or without the being, and in relation to him, if they threaten him with death, are hidden from him by the censor. If the censor is hiding the happenings which threaten the being with death, it has particular reason to hide the actual death of the being. If the man learns of his own death, than he won't fall into psychosis or depression, but

THE RECCURENT ACTION OF THAT INFORMATION WOULD IMMEDIATELY DESTROY THE BEING OR FORCE IT TO SUICIDE

[2] Carl G. Jung: "Man and his symbols" p.63, Zagreb 1973

OR WOULD THROW IT INTO PSYCHOLOGICAL MADNESS.

In this is the essence of the subconsciouss conflict between life and death within man himself. In this conflict, the censor, (an element of the intuition), doesn't allow that which is life in man, (also in flora nad fauna) to have contact with the disorganization of the organism, i.e., with death.

Because no single living being is able to live within death itself, their censors alienate them from death in the relative eternity of their species through reproductive energy. This process is TOTAL NEGATION OF DEATH, the opposite to the TOTAL NEGATION OF LIFE on death's side. Thus, in man – the spermatozoid, and in woman – the fertile cell – is contained the eternity of the species, i.e., the eternity of the individual, regardless of whether they fertilize or not. Therefore, subconsciously, before death itself man cannot believe that he'll die.

With the appearance of the conscious mind and, more specifically, self-consciousness, the history of mankind begins this leads, among other things, to the unconscious self-destruction of humanity, because for the total negation of death, which is ensured by procreative energy, neither consciousness nor self-consciousness is sufficient. The relationship between consciousness and intuition enables man to separate himself from animals and plants as a special being who is conscious of his existence, of the world that surrounds him; to be aware of what is possible and impossible for him on the earthly and cosmic levels; to ask questions about his rate and to give answers. But part of the information which the conscious mind receives from the intuition threatens to be dangerous reception of information about its own future death, and, the recurrent action of that information, would immediately destroy the being or force it to suicide or would throw it into pathological madness.

But, not only this danger is leaning over us. There are two worlds for man: the worlds of his senses and the world of his intuition (or science). Science learned about the cosmos and the micro world, but all learning is only remembering, as Plato says. If the conscious will confronts the world of intuition, it will confront the world in which its aspirations, hopes, and dreams mean nothing. The man subconsciously desires the world of science (intuition) to stay secret, because, if he confronts it, the recurrent action of that confrontation, would immediately kill the being or force it to suicide or would throw it into pathological madness. Therefore, the danger is when the intuitive knowledge becomes conscious knowledge.

The censor found the way out of this danger or consciousness: FROM CORPORAL AND NONCORPORAL OBJECTS WHICH ARE CONSICOUSLY KNOWN, IT ABSTRACTS THE DIRECT CONTRADICTION OF DEATH – ETERNITY, and thus alienates the consciousness in eternity so that it does not have to confront its own death; the censor's intuition contains the idea. Therefore the conscious mind is forced to admit illusions as well as reality, because of this we aren't quite sure what is irrational, and what rational in our thought and manner. This confirms Freud, because he:

> "...didn't have a high opinion of our thought system which is so characteristic of modern man in the West, on the

contrary, he believed that our conscious thinking is only a part of the totality of the psychological process which goes on in us, a part so unimportant in comparison with the great power of those forces in us, that are dark, irrational, unconscious".[3]

What those forces, so dark, irrational, and unconscious, are and what consequence they have for humanity, will see from the following exposition.

---

[3] D.T.Suzuki; E.Fromm: "Zen buddhism and psychoanalysis" p.207, Nolit, Belgrade 1964

ON THINGS WHICH DON'T EXIST IN NATURE

After the appearance of the consciousness people were excited by the stars, eclipse of the moon, the sun, earthquakes, lighting, thunder, wind, fire…and in all of that, wondering and fear were the dominant emotions. As a result of these feelings, the first abstraction was supernatural, mystical power which natural phenomena contain. People began to realize that these powers have their own will; so if the power of fertility wants, it fertilizes plants and animals, if it doesn't, it won't. If someone is killed by thunder, then for some reason, the power of the thunder has punished him. The people realized that their fate depended on the will of these mystical powers, and felt the need to pray to them, so if there was a drought, they prayed to the power of the clouds to bring rain; if the sea waves were dangerous, they prayed to the power of the sea gale to lower the height of the waves. So rituals appeared dedicated to these mystical powers. They called them: god of the underground, god of sun, god of fertility. Therefore there were many eternal gods. THE IDEA OF THE ETERNITY OF GODS DOESN'T COME

FROM KNOWLEDGE OF THEIR ETERNITY, BUT FROM MAN'S SUBCONSCIOUS IMPULS TO IDENTIFY WITH ETERNITY. The concrete of the rituals dedicated to the gods and the consciousness of them, is a guarantee for the subconscious that one's being is connected with eternity. Here it must be stressed that GODS DON'T HAVE A CORRESPONDENCE WITH NATURE, DON'T EXIST IN IT, EXCEPT IN MAN'S ABSTRACTION. With this, man involved himself in the famous triangle

MAN – RITUAL – GODS.

The passing from polytheism to monotheism is not the theme of this book, and we'll say only that that passage was a slow process, but at the same time a big event in the progress of mythological thought. The gods are now UNDERSTOOD as one god, which created and rules the world. It's very important that the mythological thought discovered that the world didn't always exist, but rather was created by the creative power – god. This god controls the rates of individuals, emperors and empires; rewards them when in a good mood, punishes them when angry, and, because of this, the combination: GOD – RITUAL – MAN IS THE SAME as within polytheism, though somewhat modified. AND, THE MONOTHEISTICAL GOD DOESN'T HAVE A CORRESPONDENCE WITH NATURE, DOESN'T EXIST IN IT, EXCEPT IN MAN'S ABSTRACTION.

For the nation we'll only say that which relates to this theme. From elements like common language, common customs, common historical past the concept "nation" is abstracted. All nationalists practice rituals dedicated to the nation. Scientific and historical works are dedicated to the nation; sports matches defend the national color. And the final ritual – self-sacrifice in war for the glory and eternity of the nation. NATION DOESN'T CORRESPONDENCE TO NATURE, DOESN'T EXIST IN IT, EXCEPT IN MAN'S ABSTRACTION. And so, man got involved in a triangular spider web:

MAN – RITUAL – NATION

All political ideologies, which have their own anthems, flags and armies, have their own celebrations, write their own histories, assign titular awards, all of which are rituals dedicated to the glory and eternity of the political ideology, as is the ritual of self-sacrifice for the political ideology. THE IDEOLOGY DOESN'T CORRESPOND TO THE NATURE, DOESN'T EXIST IN IT, EXCEPT IN MAN'S ABSTRACTION. And, so, man got involved in a muddy triangle:

MAN - RITUAL - IDEOLOGY.

Every state has its own patron: religion, nation, or ideology. Usually the patrons are double: religion and nation or ideology and nation, and one of the two enjoy certain advantages. Every state has jurisdiction, government, army, police; has health, education, scientific, artistic, sporting institutions and associations at national and international level; has agriculture, industry, trade… All these separate spheres of social activity have their own hierarchy of material fortune, power and glory from which is abstracted – SOCIAL STATUS. Hatred, envy, selfishness, intrigue, perjury, murder are dedicated to the aim of taking away the higher status of the neighbour.

These are rituals dedicated to the abstraction: SOCIAL STATUS. THE STATUS DOESN'T CORRESPOND TO NATURE, DOESN'T EXIST IN IT, EXCEPT IN MAN'S ABSTRACTION. Thus, man got involved in a triangular trap:

MAN - RITUAL – STATUS.

Man cannot but admire the genius of Dostoevsky. He could intuit the reasons and consequences of cosmic events, thus he gathered truths without which man is not in a condition to realize his own essence; one of them is the following:

> "Man does only this: he imagined god
> in order to live and not kill himself; the
> whole history so far lies in that."[4]

Dostoevsky is saying: subconsciously man imagines God and alienates himself in His eternity, and this alienation is subconsciously experienced as his own eternity, and the balance between life and death is secured and he can live without killing himself. As we see, religion is not a consequence of primitivism, ignorance, vulgarity – but of existential necessity, which operates outside the scope of the rational consciousness. Because the alienation in god helps man to live, not to kill himself, religion is a rational solution to the problem of man's existence in relation to the nature.

Religion is a unique teaching which promises life beyond the grave, this is also the main thread in the philosophy of the religious institution, and when there's about man's eternity, the discussions and the polemics revolve around

---

[4] F.M.Dostoevsky: "Devils", p.345, Moscow 1957

religion. While some played with that "eternity", and some blindly believed in it, Dostoevsky discovered the positive function of eternity in relation to man's existence.

For Marx-Engels, this "god's eternity" wasn't innocent and naïve. They thought that "eternity" was reflection of money, goods and capital and concluded:

> "...the real basis of the religious reflection has a lasting existence, and with it the religious reflex."[5]

In other words, "eternity" reflects goods, money, instruments of production because of this man has a religious relationship with this banal objects, only rituals are different and he gives them a mystic power. But, today there're many who have neither emotional nor a rational relationship with god and eternity, and for them there is no religious reflex. Meanwhile, which of those atheists isn't charmed by material fortune, or by power, or by glory, or by nation, or by ideology...or by two or more of the mentioned abstractions at the same time? None of the abstractions from the stated corporal and non-corporal objects, correspond to nature, or exist in it, nor does the imaginary god exists in it. In the earthly life, as the people sacrificed themselves for their own religion, so do they, and did they sacrifice themselves for their own nation or power. We'll now see how and why.

---

[5] F.Engels: "Anti-Düring", p.386, Culture 1964

GENESIS OF AGGRESSION

The superiority of man over man, in whatever circumstance, is one of the elements of the genesis of aggression, so let's look at it closely.

If we put a man and a woman with their ton of gold and diamonds in the position of Adam and Eve, i.e., lonely on some desert island, will their fortune mean anything to them? It will count for nothing, because fortune is "sweet", only when it's looked at it with the eyes of the poor. If we isolate someone with great power and the highest glory from the people, the power and the glory will mean nothing to him, because he won't have anyone to rule over, he won't anyone to reflect his glory. For superiority to appear two people are needed. For an isolated man like this one, neither nation, nor religion, nor ideology, would mean anything at all, because he would have no one to whom, with "history", "philosophy", "science" and art, he could demonstrate the SUPREMACY of his own nation, religion or ideology over those of the neighbours. He wouldn't have anyone to fight, in order to realize the supremacy of his own religion, nation, ideology over those of the neighbours. Children have no idea of what nation, religion or ideology is, even so they become nationalists, pilgrims, ideologists; listening at home and at school for the SUPREMACY of their own nation, religion or ideology over that of the neighbours. Decorations for heroism, eternal glory for holy victims… ,for what cause there is no need to know. GLORY, FORTUNE AND POWER ARE NOT ESSENTIAL TO THE PEOPLE, NEITHER IS THE NATION, RELIGION OR IDEOLOGY. BUT S U P R E M A C Y OVER THE NEIGHBOURS IN THESE RELATIVE VALUES IS.

Supremacy is neither food nor drink, nor is it useful for learning the world that surrounds us; for supremacy itself man has no concrete use. Even so, people experience it with it gaiety, joy, optimism, happiness, delight…,and when we lose supremacy, we meet sorrow, frustration, care, depression, fear…How can supremacy, which is usually achieved by aggression, and therefore immorally, cause appearance of so lifegiving emotions like gaiety, joy, happiness, delight…? Some claim that the supremacy of man over man is the motivating force in the progress of humanity.

Different to the conscious supremacy of man over man in power or nation is the intuitive impulse towards unconscious supremacy. Namely: from birth to the end of life, death constantly "fights" against the life of man, and life is constantly protecting itself:

on the organic level with the immunity, reflexes, senses, instincts;

on the psychological level with life's symbols – eternity, against the symbol of death – nothingness;

in man a subconscious "war" for the supremacy of life over death is continually fought.

Now, if the conscious and subconscious supremacy depend on each other in relation to the fate of the being itself, than we are at the threshold of discovery of aggression, and if they are not related, the genesis of aggression stays secret.

There're many scientific works which talk about the informative relation between the subconscious (intuition) and the conscious mind, and that means that the subconscious and the conscious minds are DEPENDENT on each other in relation to the fate of the being itself. Information from the intuition (or subconscious) serves the conscious mind for orientation, working, studying, creation and information from the conscious mind is remade, transformed into symbol* necessary for human existence, and symbol which negates existence by the subconscious. Let's see, what these symbols are. Jung says:

> A word or picture is symbolic when it contains something more than the apparent direct meaning."[6]

So, for instance:

> power - more than power - lordship, power - less than power - slavery; people - more than people - nation, people - less than people - herd,...

"Herd" is a mocking word when it's related to a group of people. He adds further:

---

[6] C.G.Jung: "Man and his symbols" p.20, Zagreb 1973
*Signs are related to things which exist in nature, and symbols are related to things which don't exist in nature

> "Even (the symbol) may become something completely different when it's involved in the subconscious." [7]

It's obvious, says Jung, that in the conscious mind the symbol means one thing and in the subconscious another:

> "It (the symbol) has a wider unconscious form, which is never exactly determined or totally explained. And one can't hope that one will be able to determine or explain it." [8]

Let's try to determine and explain it ourselves.

Above all, symbols form themselves in the subconscious and have nothing to relate to, except life and death in the man which they form. That means that they also relate to the conflict between life and death within that man. We realized that the confrontation between consciousness and death is deadly; organic life can't "fight" against death, because death is disorganization, entropy of organic life. Therefore symbols act against death in confrontation between consciousness and death.

Now we can go back to Jung's psychological axiom: he symbol may become something completely different when it's involved in the subconscious. This axiom says, that some symbols are known to us, some are unknown. For instance, the symbols nation, god, ideology, lordship and glory are known to us, but when they're involved in the subconscious, they lose their main meaning and become something COMPLETELY DIFFERENT. This COMPLETE DIFFERENCE must result from the

---

[7] C.G.Jung: "Man and his symbols" p.43, Zagreb 1973
[8] C.G.Jung: "Man and his symbols" p.20, Zagreb 1973

conflict between life and death within man himself, and every known symbol in the subconscious develops into ETERNITY, like life's symbol, and in NOTHINGNESS, like death's symbol.

This is proved in dreams by the symbols which, actually, are picture of the dreamer's state in relation to life and death, i.e., are narrating the real autobiography. THE SYMBOLS OF WHICH WE ARE AWARE AND THOSE OF WHICH WE ARE UNAWARE, DEVELOP FROM THESE TWO MAIN SYMBOLS: ETERNITY AND NOTHINGNESS, and the conflict between organic life and organic death is fought on the psychological level between the symbols of eternity and nothingness. Thus, if someone dream with a picture (symbol) of a funeral (which develops from the main symbol – nothingness), foresees the death of the dreamer, Freud's symbol converts the funeral to marriage (which develops from the main symbol – eternity) to protect the dreamer from depression, fear or psychological trauma, i.e., it disconnects the contact between the conscious mind and death. Here we must say that: FOR THE CONSCIOUSNESS, THE PICTURES, THE WORDS OR THE NUMBERS IN THE DREAM ARE SIGNS, AND FOR THE SUBCONSCIOUS SYMBOLS. I think that we determined and explained the main function of the symbols which are involved in the subconscious.

Let's return to the mutual dependence of the conscious and subconscious supremacy.

THE IMPULSE OF THE UNCONSCIOUS SUPREMACY OF ETERNITY OVER NOTHINGNESS DETERMINES THE

CONSCIOUS SUPREMACY OF MAN OVER MAN IN ALL SITUATIONS, and

THE CONSCIOUS SUPREMACY OF MAN OVER MAN, REFLECTING ITSELF IN THE SUBCONSCIOUS, ENSURES THE SUPREMACY OF ETERNITY OVER NOTHINGNESS.

Now, let's remind ourselves of the remarkable Dostoevsky's axiom, which has an immediate connection with conscious and unconscious supremacy. The axiom is: 'generally, in every misfortune of the neighbour there is something gay in the eyes that look on – who ever you are". A humane man, although he will pity the unfortune, will be pierced by either obvious or hidden joy. Is the neighbour disaster itself evoking the appearance of joy? Surely, no. From this disaster no one gets rich, neither spiritually, nor materially. Maybe, because of conscious supremacy over the unfortunate, the happiness is supreme over the disaster. But man doesn't get rich, either spiritually or materially, from this supremacy either. Sometimes I play chess with a neighbour of mine. When he check mates me he's delighted, happy as a child, and when I check mate him he's embarrassed and almost starts to cry. Why is this neighbour happy when he gets nothing, and embarrassed when he loses nothing? And who doesn't react more or less like him? No one. Something essential is happening here:

Conscious supremacy, reflecting itself in the subconscious, is ensuring the supremacy of eternity over nothingness, at the same time, it is SUBCONSCIOUS CONTACT WITH ETERNITY, and this contact causes the appearance of gaiety, joy, happiness…,and vice versa.

Conscious humbleness or insult, reflecting itself in the subconscious, ensures unconscious supremacy of nothingness over eternity, at the same time, it is UNCONSCIOUS CONTACT WITH NOTHINGNESS, and this contact results in the appearance of sorrow, fear, depression, psychological trauma.

Jesus said:

> "He who doesn't know what water is, knows nothing."[9]

In his style, I say: he who doesn't understand that the ORIGIN OF EMOTIONS IS IN SUBCONSCIOUS CONTACT WITH LIFE AND DEATH THROUGH THEIR SYMBOLS ETERNITY AND NOTHINGNESS, has nothing to say about man.

Now we can define the genesis of aggression.

THE GENESIS OF AGGRESSION IS IN THE SUBCONSCIOUS CONFLICT BETWEEN LIFE AND DEATH, WHICH IS CHARACTERIZED BY THE SUBCONSCIOUS SUPREMACY OF ETERNITY (as symbol of life) OVER NOTHINGNESS (as death's symbol); THIS UNCONSCIOUS SUPREMACY DETERMINES CONSCIOUS SUPREMACY OF MAN OVER MAN IN ALL SITUATIONS, WHICH IS ENSURED MAINLY BY ACTIVE AGGRESSION.

This means that people don't hate each other, don't envy each other, don't perjury against each other and don't kill each other individually, but as members of a group, and therefore in massive number, because of power, glory,

---

[9] Elaine Pagels: "Gnostic gospels" p.162, Belgrade 1981

fortune,...nor because they wish to be supreme in these relevant valueless constructs, - but because of eternity, by which death is negated, without which man is not in a condition to live. This eternity, as we have seen, is ensured by aggression.

RITUAL AND NATIONAL CONSCIOUSNESS

Now, let's face a truth: neither religion, nation or ideology exist in nature, neither power, glory nor material fortune exist in nature; freedom, brotherhood, equality and slavery, division, inequality, have no existence I nature. Man cannot sow and reap, cannot make clothes and bedclothes, cannot make homes, bridges, vehicles, cannot learn about the universe and about himself, cannot reproduce himself with these abstractions. But because these abstractions give man supremacy over man, people hate each other, envy each other, though the abstractions have no concrete use.

This undoubtedly confirms Freud's opinion: dark, irrational, and at the same time unconscious powers rule man. It is certain that those are powers that are contradictory to rational powers: the rational powers build, the irrational ones destroy; the rational powers try to order societies, the irrational ones create chaos. Exactly what are those dark, irrational, unconscious powers? We already know them. They are: ritual feeling, ritual knowledge, ritual consciousness, ritual life dedicated to abstractions which do not correspond to nature; don't exist in it, except within man. They are: religion, nation, ideology; freedom and slavery, brotherhood and division, equality and inequality; power, glory and material fortune.

Practicing rituals dedicated to the above abstractions, man transforms himself from a concrete into an abstract being, i.e., into a national, ideological, religious, powerful, glorious or rich being. Not small number of people spend their whole lives under the banner of one, two, three or more, abstractions. If, for instance, you meet a man who lives under the symbol "nation", he will tell you "remarkable" details from the history of his nation, stressing the heroic victories and defeats on battle fields; will pour out his hatred for bordering nations, will introduce you to the immortal portrays of dukes and national scientist and artists. The national-ritual consciousness also falls into that kind of national madness, so that even the mountains, rivers and trees are decorated in the national colour. He will narrate all that to you, to prove the supremacy of his own nation over his neighbours'.

The wish, the longing, for his nation to be supreme over the bordering nations are – ritual feelings.

The ideas with which they find a way to keep or to acquire the supremacy to their own over bordering nations is – ritual thought.

Knowledge of the supremacy of their own nation over other nations is – ritual knowledge.

Consciousness of the ritual knowledge is – ritual consciousness.

Ritual feelings, ritual thought, ritual knowledge, ritual consciousness combined form – ritual life.

It's obvious that the national being contradicts its own nature. Its ritual life alienates it from nature, and nature has no value for the being; for it a subject of another nation is not part of nature, but a monster which should be destroyed. If doesn't that, it itself is a monster. The same thing is true of religious, ideological, powerful or glorious beings.

Ritual consciousness, knowledge, feeling, thought, life have nothing in common with the laws of nature and with nature itself. They avoid questions like the origin of the cosmos, of life, of the earth and everything that is on it; they are not attracted by the acquisition of food, clothes or homes or even of knowledge of this world which surrounds us. But besides all the destruction caused by ritual consciousness and knowledge they have a major role in keeping human kind in existence, because the conscious rituals dedicated to the nation, power or glory in the subconscious mean keeping a relationship with eternity, without which the man isn't in a condition to live.

The most remarkable product of rational consciousness is mathematics. We meet it in formulae which correspond to nature, particularly to the laws of nature. It is an expression of the four dimensions of bodies, of aggregate states and the internal and external movement in space. With mathematics, i.e., with rational consciousness, man pursues an abstract relationship with things which correspond to nature; exist in it. Acting with mathematics, man transforms nature in accordance with his existential and spiritual needs. Mathematics even created the possibility of creating new material elements, like trans-uranic, for example. Thanks to mathematics, man creates robots which are changing the physical labour more and more, and what is more important, physical labour which is dangerous for the health. Rational consciousness has brought humanity to the point of a grand technological revolution which will open possibilities for creating a far more delightful heaven on Earth, than the heavens of all religious together.

But beside the truly great possibilities of rational consciousness, let's face its only negative characteristic. Well discuss it, beginning with a quotation from Dostoevsky:

> "Freedom and the free mind and science will seduce them into such impasses and will put them in the face of such miracles and unsolvable mysteries, that some of them will disobediently and violently destroy themselves, the other, disobedient an less powerful, ones will destroy each other, and the third, the wretched, will grovel at our feet and burst out sobbing: save us from ourselves."[10]

This is said by "The grand inquisitor". He believes that the freedom which Jesus left like a message to humanity is something that one billion people aren't in a condition to understand or to live with, and that that freedom is a privilege for one million people: Jesus' chosen men. The teaching of "The grand inquisitor" is salvation for a billion people.

"The grand inquisitor" is protecting his own power, but is also justifying his disappointment with Jesus' teaching. Explaining the complications and the dangers of freedom, he says:

---

[10] F.M.Dostoevsky: "The grand inquisitor" in "Brothers Karamazov"

> "Calmness, even death, is dearer to man,
> than a free choice between good and evil.
> There is nothing more tempting for man
> than the freedom of his conscience, but
> there's nothing harder."[11]

When man starts to live according to his own "free choice" he'll discover that:

> "The mystery for the human being isn't
> why he lives, but this: for what he's living.
> Without a clear picture of what his life
> is for, man will not agree to live and he'd
> commit suicide rather than stay on Earth,
> even though there he would be surrounded
> with white bread." [12]

It's obvious that "The grand inquisitor" doesn't find happiness in "the free choice between good and evil", i.e., in freedom, nor in the "clear picture of life", i.e., in rational consciousness, but in the nature of things themselves, the basis of which is: a satisfied stomach, a roof over your head, clothes, games and procreation. That is what fills him with naïve, childish gaiety; he doesn't have other happiness. A billion people could live like this, and not desire "free choice between good and evil" and a "clear picture of the life", keeps them charmed with MIRACLES, SECRETS and AUTHORITY, and this duty is fulfilled by a million people, who govern them directly. This billion people will produce goods for existence, but because of greed and egoism won't be able to share their fortune among

---

[11] F.M. Dostoevsky: "The grand inquisitor" from "Brothers Karamazov"
[12] F.M. Dostoevsky: "The grand inquisitor" from "Brothers Karamazov"

themselves without provoking disorder. Therefore, THE AUTHORITY will take away the products and, will return to families what they need, keeping the surplus. Because of this, people will obey and admire AUTHORITY, for it liberated them from, to them, the unsolved problem of how to share the fortune. My "free choice" will always be to my benefit, but not to my neighbours' benefit as well.

This is "The grand inquisitor" vision of then human order. Here it ought to be stressed that it refers the future. The time still hadn't come, when "the clear picture of the life" would determine the fate of the people. We have seen that "The grand inquisitor" attacks liberty, the free mind and science, and this means that he attacks rational consciousness, because freedom and rational consciousness lead humanity to suicide.

It's understood that the philosophy of "The grand inquisitor" has no basis. Ritual consciousness had already brought humanity face to face with suicide, before rational consciousness could do that. All of what was and is known about freedom and slavery, about the rational and the irrational, is completely wrong and unproved. We have already talked about the danger of rational consciousness, but because of the importance of this problem, we must repeat it with an extended text.

Scientific (rational) knowledge discloses to the conscious mind the disorganization of organic beings, therefore of man also, so when that discovery reaches a critical point, its recurrent action will destroy the being immediately or will force it to suicide or will throw it in pathological madness. This is one of the dangers of rational consciousness. The second danger follows:

Man's picture of the world that surrounds him is formed, generally, from the data of the senses. We watch the far away stars, stages of the moon, feel the light and warmth of the sun, admire the colour's game and fear thunder, fires, floods, earthquakes and strong winds. We sail, swim and fish in the rivers, lakes and seas; smell and taste parts of the Earth, and use plants and animals for eating. These are all conditions for life which man finds in the earthly world. In the earthly world we reproduce ourselves, we find our reason for gaiety, happiness, sorrow and fear; the blue sky makes us cheerful, darkness come with dreaming. Man feels and knows, that without this earthly world he cannot exist; he sprouted on this world, he knows it and doesn't fear it, because it is the measure of his soul.

Meanwhile, the world of science or intuition, isn't like this earthly world in which man finds much of value to him, in which he feels secure, where he walks on paths of optimism. The world of science isn't for dimensional, but very much more dimensional. There are many existential contradictions between man as an organic being and the many-dimensional world, and the more man discovers it, the more his information weighs on him, that is to say, man has no chance in this unimaginably vast, endless world, in which the sad destiny of the earthly world is curved out, which will one day turn itself to dust. And when the weight of his information about this strange, unknown, dangerous world reaches a critical point, the recurrent action of the information will immediately destroy the being, or force it to suicide, or throw it in pathological madness. The corporal and psychological possibilities of man thrive on this earthly world, are adapted to it, and every rational move away into vast, amazing world, which are contradictory to this earthly world, presents certain risks.

Rational consciousness and knowledge, by discovering technological possibilities, make life easier, more comfortable, more spectacular, but, they also discover that world, which has nothing to offer but death. For this reason they are a potential danger to human kind.

ALIENATION AND INALIENATION

We are now acquainted with two desperate consciousnesses: rational and ritual.

Functionally, ritual consciousness is – ALIENATION. Alienation in symbols like: god, nation, ideology, justice, glory, lordship and liberty. We are aware of the rituals that we dedicate to these symbols, but we aren't aware (or we weren't aware until now), of what determines the form of alienation. With alienation on god, man objectifies himself as a national being. Why does man objectify his being in an abstraction which is contradictory to his natural being? Because the natural being is mortal, but the religious or national being is "eternal". With alienation in symbols like god or nation, which in the subconscious develop into eternity, the being also develops into eternity. This means that in objectifying himself consciously as a glorious or ideological being he's subconsciously objectifying himself as an eternal being. This identification with eternity gives man psychological immunity which protects him from that deadly infection – inalienation. He who doesn't understand, isn't in a condition to live with death within himself, nor does he understand the function of alienation. Therefore people subconsciously identify with beings contradictory to their natural beings.

Rational consciousness functionally is – INALIENATION. Admitting the laws of nature as a basic truth, upon which it leans and from which it starts, rational consciousness is constantly correcting its understanding of the world, which is all the more commensurate with the laws themselves. Thus we have two worlds: the world of feelings, which is irrational, and the world of natural laws which is rational. Feelings are not in contact with the laws of nature, but they have a rational role in the life of beings, though the world which they show doesn't correspond to the truth, i.e., it's irrational. What would man be if he didn't look, hear, taste, smell, touch? Of course he wouldn't exist. Throwing away the world of feelings, the rational consciousness puts itself into conflict with its own feelings, and here begins the delusion of rational consciousness in relation to its own being.

Rational consciousness cannot reconcile itself with the alienation of being in fictitious eternities. As we saw, alienation on god, nation, ideology, power, glory or status is actually alienation in eternity. For rational consciousness that is fraudulent, because every organic being is mortal. Meanwhile, the nation alienates the being in eternity, in order to obstruct the contact of rational consciousness with its own death, because

INALIENATION LEADS TO ALIENATION FROM THE BEING ITSELF,

and that means suicide, mutual self-destruction, i.e., chaos, which humanity can't even imagine. We come to the paradox of paradoxes: in relation to man's existence

RITUAL CONSCIOUSNESS ACTS RATIONALLY, AND RATIONAL CONSCIOUSNESS ACTS IRRATIONALLY.

It's obvious that in relation to the existence to human kind, rational consciousness is more dangerous than ritual consciousness, but technological progress gave ritual consciousness a weapon with which it can destroy humanity several times. With this,

THE DANGER OF ALIENATION HAS EQUALED THE DANGER OF INALIENATION.

At the moment nature preserves humanity from self-extermination with a psychological "fossil" from humanity's prehistory:

FEAR OF COMPLETE SELF-DESTRUCTION.

Where are the religious, scientific, ideological ethics? What are scientific learning, philosophical wisdom, the art aesthetic doing? How can they allow fear, which has absolutely no ethical wisdom, to preserve humanity from suicide, while they passively observe their own defeat in the face of fear? Or is that feeling "fear"* some growing awareness of a form which appears from the depths of nature? Isn't that presentiment knowledge which nature, not the individual, possesses? And isn't the culture of nature far above the culture of our ritual and rational consciousness?

But will this fear be ever stronger because of desire for the supremacy of my religion, your nation, his ideology? Because of the glory and eternity of these abstractions people even sacrificed their own lives, so the whole of humanity can be sacrificed. The logic of events suggests

---

*Feelings are the knowledge of biological nature

this assumption to us: if the spirit of man had some role in cosmic events, and that role is about to bring the curtain down on humanity, then the humanity will destroy itself. I pray to God it won't be like that.

The very fact that humanity has brought itself to the brink of self-extermination, undoubtedly confirms that both ritual and rational consciousness and knowledge are defective. Even if humanity does not destroy itself in the future, it's possible that people will continue to live emptily, wastefully, in disgust; wandering in the foggy triangle:

MAN- ALIENATION –INALIENATION

As ritual and rational beings, until they bring themselves face to face with suicide again, because neither ritual nor rational consciousness has anything to offer them.

Well, is there some other consciousness or knowledge that could free us from this destructive behaviour? Some say that there is no other consciousness, knowledge, intellect or mind. Some say that this consciousness, intellect, mind, that is somewhat known to us is the extended arm of the cosmic intellect, mind, consciousness. I belong to the second group.

So far we have shown, that the chaos in relations between people is determined by the bio-psychological canon, and the vital question is: can we change this canon for another biological canon, one which will lead to symmetry, harmony and order in the life of humanity? The second part of this book deals with this question.

WHAT IS CONSCIOUSNESS?

Catching consciousness in action:

After the Second World War in Yugoslavia a group of citizens were set in a row to be shot. On the command "shoot" one German soldier threw his gun at his feet, though he was sure that, because of his disobedience, he would be shot, and would be shot the citizens anyhow. The soldier was shot immediately.

As do all others, this soldier could justify himself: my life is dearer to me than others' lives. But, for this soldier, the lives of others were as dear to him as his own, and he died with them. He was not able to forsake SOMETHING within him, even when it offered him death. It's obvious that there are men who are freed by that SOMETHING from the fear of death.

Here is another example: seven hundred years ago (I don't know precisely), for the first time existential labour was brought in into a Buddhist temple. A certain Mr. Hiacugo founded a monastery for Zen Buddhist monks. One of the rules of the house order was that all monks, including the teacher, must practice existential labour.

"Even when he got old, Hiacugo refused to stop gardening. Worried about his passing years, his disciples hid his gardening tools, so that he wouldn't exhaust himself working. But Hiacugo said to them: "IF I DON'T WORK, I WON'T EAT".[13]

This statement: if I don't work, I won't eat, - has two aspects.

The first aspect is ethical and is based upon freedom, brotherhood and equality. These are abstractions which appeared as reactions to slavery, division and inequality in rights and duties. Hiacugo said this to them: if I don't ensure my existence with my own existential labour, I'm taking away my neighbours' freedom, making a division between me and them, and I'm supporting the rights of the powerful over the weak and the insulted. Therefore, I would gladly die of hunger rather than do it.

Actually, a predisposition to freedom, brotherhood and equality was always present as an ideal for societies, in the form of desire and action expressed in peasant risings and sociological revolutions. But, freedom, justice and equality were never and nowhere realized, because, after victory, the victors became conquerors.

The second aspect is, the symmetry, harmony and order which are shown in the laws of the cosmos as it is, with possibilities open for revolution. Just as there are men who subconsciously relate more intensely to the principles which relate to colours, tones and numbers and become painters, composers or inventors; there are men who subconsciously feel more intensely the whole order

---

[13] D.T.Suzuki. E.Fromm: "Zen Buddhism and psychoanalysis", p.94, Nolit 1964

of the cosmos, and become CONSCIOUS BEINGS, i.e., they relate symmetrically, harmoniously and properly to their neighbours, even, when they have to sacrifice their own lives. And what frees them from the fear of death? The most likely possibility is this:

The people who feel the symmetry, harmony and order in the cosmos intensely and deeply, are also feeling the cosmic SPIRIT, which maintains that order, symmetry and harmony. Its eternity feels like their own, so they don't even recognize personal death; for them death doesn't exist. Maybe the poet gives the real picture of the cosmic spirit here:

> "As soon as the darkness lights the stars, there appears an abyss with a SUPERIOR "from-to".
> If we diminish this infinity, we are coming to an INFERIOR "from-to".
> The length of all directions means nothing in Space.
> The infinite large and the infinite small, converging into ONE, do make the cosmic SPIRIT,
> Which, therefore, spreads in every point of the abyss.

Man's spirit is partly composed of the cosmic SPIRIT, therefore: SPIRIT IS NOT FOUND IN THE BODY, but, THE BODY IS FOUND IN THE COSMIC SPIRIT. Therefore, man's death is the separation of the body from the spirit, by which process, the spirit contains both the external and internal shapes of the body, reflected in the spirit. This is neither fantasy nor mystic fable. A parapsychologist wanted to surprise a close friend of his, and he concentrated his thought on his being in an armchair beside his friend's chimney and he felt asleep, exhausted. For ten to fifteen minutes the friend spoke to the vision. The next day, the friend was surprised to hear that he had been talking to a vision. This means that before the death also the spirit separate itself from the body. "Double" by Dostoevsky, is one of the most starlit books in world literature, exactly, for this reason, because he describes the real relation of Goliatkin to his vision.

Freedom, brotherhood, equality, right, justice and humanity, as man has imagined them, don't correspond to the nature, therefore man has nothing with which to realize them. However, symmetry, harmony and order are in the essence of nature itself. The problem is to spread cosmic symmetry, harmony and order into human relations. This can be realized if chaotic beings are transformed into conscious beings. The most serious obstacle to this transformation is the fear of death.

The fear of death is accepted as a natural reality, which is confirmed by obvious arguments, so that " having no fear of death" is considered to be something unnatural and impossible. Therefore, not one psychologist, philosopher or writer...has taken the "having the fear of death" as an object for observation. But, the case of the German soldier or of Hiacugo, who are not, surely, lonely, calls that "having no fear of death" is dependent on the spiritual relationship of man with nature, to which we must pay attention.

Someone, whose moustaches was yet to appear, asked the advise of his illiterate mother, decorating it in a poetic mantle. Here's the advice:

> "Son, if something happens to you, which
> frees you from the fear of death, also if

you're as poor as e beggar, powerless,
humble, insulted, glory eludes you, you are
made mad, if you are not afraid of death,
you have the greatest power, your power
darkens the power of all crowns, you are
wiser than all learned man in this world,
because there is no greater power, glory
and wisdom than that by which is clamed
death.

Actually, this mother as tried to say: wisdom, glory and power, which are relevant up to death, mean nothing in nature and have no value; and in that wisdom, power and glory, which spread into infinity, till birth and after the grave, consists the sap of life. Now we can define consciousness:

CONSCIOUSNESS IS SUBCONSCIOUS LEARNING WHOSE PROPENSITY IS TO EXTEND COSMIC SYMMETRY, HARMONY, ORDER INTO RELATION AMONG PEOPLE.

But you are foisting life beyond grave on us, - thus orthodox atheists would react, for whom atheism is law. I think that in this observation on consciousness there is neither mysticism nor fantasy and that I'm using ideas which correspond to nature, and ideas for which there are logical assumptions, which correspond to nature. But let's see, do atheists really exist?

The atheist knows that God, of whichever religious institution, doesn't exist, and life beyond the grave doesn't exist for any man. This learning, dogma for many atheists, develops into cults, which contains religious characteristics. Meanwhile, alienation on god has the same function, as does alienation in nation, ideology, glory, government or cult – the securing of individual eternity. And which atheist doesn't belong to a nation, or political ideology; which atheist doesn't yearn after power, glory or material fortune? As we see, there are no atheists. The only atheist in humanity so far is – Jesus.

Negating life after death, the atheists are offering humanity nothing. The hope for a happy tomorrow comes from the subconscious belief in eternal life; the perspectives from which we are looking at the prosperity of humanity come from our subconscious belief in life beyond the grave. If man confronts his own personal death, for what will be hope, of what use will the perspectives be? With death within him, can man dream that he will raise himself through science or art? Of course not. Confronted with death, can man feel gaiety, joy, happiness? In no way! Gaiety, joy are results of subconscious contact with personal eternity. Well see, you atheist, when you have feelings of gaiety or joy, it's because of this: you subconsciously believe in personal eternity, in personal life beyond the grave.

A UNIQUE WAY OUT

We saw that conscious aggression among man is a consequence of the natural canon, which is universal, except for conscious people.

Conscious people don't lie, don't steal, even when hunger threatens death, and don't kill.

They don't know what pride, hatred, envy, anger or revenge are.

When insulted, they don't react with insults, if they are injured they don't require revenge.

They don't feel superior to their neighbours in anything.

They don't desire power, glory, material fortune and don't participate in any nation, political ideology or religious institutions.

They don't attack the integrity of their neighbours, and are not indifferent when someone else does it.

Their own existences are ensured by personal labour; producing goods for existence, producing health and knowledge.

If someone is a leader in something, he's in no way separated from the group that he leads.

And they do not fear death.

This is an unfinished moral portrait of conscious people. A unique way out of the chaos in human relations is: THE TRANSFORMATION OF MAN FROM AN AGGRESSIVE INTO A COSNCIOUS BEING. To encourage this transformation, radical economic-legislative changes are necessary. These changes are related to sex and labor.

TWO ASPECTS OF SEX

The first aspect is economic. The Earth doesn't have unlimited space for settling, nor has it unlimited space for agriculture. India did everything to stop hunger, but the birth of two hundred million new stomachs has prolonged the presence of hunger. China managed to bring down the population to number for which its territory is adequate, allowing for infertile years as well. Bravo, China! A rising population brings with it a rising number of factories and cities and cuts down the space for agriculture. And so on. It's necessary to know that every third child in a family is a child of hunger.

The second aspect is psychological. Racial, national, religious and class prejudice also have infected sex. If a young white man marries black girl and vice versa, he exposes himself to insult and boycott. The same is true, to e greater or lesser extent, with boys and girls from different religions, nations and classes. Procreative power (sex), doesn't separate people into races, nations, religions or classes; that's done by the different cultures and traditions. If we want to have symmetrical harmonious relations with sex, than we must not allow religious, national, racial or class prejudices to influence it.

I think my account is sufficient to show, how much we degrade and insult ourselves, exposing the sexual organs in disgusting curses, in the prostitute market like cattle, and by mocking denial of the points of view of different cultures and traditions. That stops us from approaching sex as a natural power, which shapes plants and animals, even the stars, because old faces die and new ones are born, and that is done by precisely this procreative power.

THREE ASPECTS OF LABOUR

Existential labour. This labour already is a factor without which the existence of humanity isn't possible. As much as man depends on nature, that much is he dependent on existential labour. This means that in relation to human existence, this labour is equal to nature. We can say without indecisiveness: for man to exist, three activities are needed:

1. To be born.
2. To produce goods needed for existence and to use them.
3. To alienate himself in a fictitious or a real eternity.

This degraded and insulted labour is the biggest and the most essential value, not just it makes it possible TO BE, which is it's primary function, but also because only upon its basis can we decide HOW TO BE. Because of this, only in existential labour can man have total satisfaction in his historical existence. The fact that existential labour is obligatory calls every individual to have a concrete relationship with existential labour, i.e., every human individual must participate in it or in some of its useful organizations. As long as the economic-legislative reconstruction of humanity doesn't charge man with this participation, aggression will be present, because alienation from existential labour isn't possible without power over, and violence towards, one's neighbour.

The origin of existential labour is in creative labour: creative labour discovers the procedure, and the existential labour repeats it in the circle of production.

Existential labour is practiced by those who are constrained, in order to survive. The prostitute sells her sexual organs, and the labourer his physical strength, and so, both sex and labour are dishonoured. There are many male and female labourers whose positions are typical slavery.

> "The empire of freedom actually begins exactly where labour determined by hardships and the realization of external goals governed by the nature of things stops. That means it (the empire of freedom) lies on the other side to the domain of production itself."[14]

Further, Marx treats existential labour as an "empire of necessity", and continues:

> "From the other side of it (existential labour) the development of man's power begins, which is an aim in itself, real empire of freedom, but which can only thrive with the empire of necessity as its basis. The shortness of the working day is the first principle."[15]

---

[14] K.Marx: "Das Kapital", p.1816, Prosveta 1973
[15] K.Marx: "Das Kapital:, p. 1816 Prosveta 1973

It's obvious, Marx claims, that existential labour is slavery; but, because humanity can't exist without it, he understands it as an "empire of necessity". From the ontological point of view existential labour is necessity, but also not labour; from the classic point of view, the producers are not slaves of labour, but of the political system.

The thought that man is created by labour, i.e., that labour has differentiated him from flora and fauna is a naïve illusion, because it means that labour has created intuition, the source of all creation. That order-of-things which creates intuition, also creates labour. Here the law itself of the nature is enriched by a new canon; a statute of creation above man.

For Jesus "God's empire" is the natural order-of-things. Explaining this empire, he says:

> "But when the fruit is brought forth, immediately he (order-of-things) putteth in the sickle, because the harvest is come."[16]

According to that, labour isn't an "Empire of necessity", which man must suffer, labour is the result of the empire of natural evolution in which man is also included over labour. Therefore, the only satisfaction for historical existence is the practicing of existential and creative labour. The spiritual play which comes from existential, creative labour and sex is a crown of life.

Marx talks about the "empire of freedom". What kind of freedom can man have, carrying within him the "empire of death"? If subconsciously or consciously man discovers the "kingdom of death", the recurrent action of that discovery

---

[16] The Gospel according to St.Marc. 4/29

will immediately destroy his being. Therefore, man is not in a state to live without the "empire of eternity". There's no "empire of freedom" without an "empire of eternity".

Finally, we can say: EXISTENTIAL LABOUR RELATES TO THINGS WHICH CORRESPOND TO NATURE, AND EXIST IN IT.

Ritual labour. Concretely, what is ritual labour?

In religious institutions ritual labour is: prayers dedicated to God; celebrating the patron of this or that church; prayers made to God at baptisms, marriages and funerals; ensuring heaven for the souls of the departed; protecting one's own religion from negation by other religions, working for expansion for one's own religion, even with weapons if necessary, sacrificing oneself for the supremacy of one's own religion over others.

In national institutions rituals are: celebrating the day of the founder of the nation; respecting the flag and the anthem of the nation; adding a national character to learned man and artists of world stature; writing national histories, dedicating songs and prose to national heroes to make the nation immortal; defending the national colour at sports matches and sacrificing oneself in wars for the glory and eternity of the nation.

In political ideologies ritual is: propaganda which protects the interests of one's own ideology; denying the realization of the goals of foreign ideologies, boasting of the realization of the goals of one's own; expression and confirmation of fidelity to the flag and anthem of the ideology; sacrificing oneself for the glory and eternity of the ideology.

For power, material fortune and glory, labour is used in science, art, sport, and in every profession, to reach a higher rank in the hierarchy of power, material fortune or glory. Intriguing, insinuating, perjuring oneself and killing to gain some high status is ritual labour. Theft for greater material fortune and higher glory is ritual labour.

Let's emphasize this: RITUAL LABOUR IS PRACTISING RELATIONS WITH THINGS THAT DON'T CORRESPOND TO NATURE, AND DON'T EXIST IN IT, EXCEPT IN MAN, AS A SYMBOL.

Creative labour finds the unknown by fumbling. It is a dynamic naughty boy which senses the hidden micro elements, and concealed macro world. It's a power which incites surprise, wonder, admiration, but also fear and disappointment. It gives impetus to progress in scientific knowledge and gives structure to technology, agronomy and medicine, but at the same time it serves aggression, as it does peace. It opens the possibility of building heaven on Earth, and the possibility of turning the earth into dust and ashes. Man wouldn't just destroy his own values, but maybe also that unique value in the cosmos – life on earth.

Through history, creative labour has changed the Earth's matter according to man's own bodily and spiritual needs; today it becomes imperative to change man himself, who has, since "Adam and Eve", stayed unchanged, the same. The dialectic of his change is transformation from an aggressive to a peaceful being.

Let's add that: CREATIVE LABOUR HAS AN ABSTRACT AND A CONCRETE RELATION TO THINGS WHICH CORRESPOND TO NATURE AND EXIST IN IT.

Because these related labours fill most of life, we'll remind ourselves of some of their characteristics in relation to humanity. The quantity of people engaged in these three forms of labour is like this:

Creative labour is practiced by the smallest number of people with a decided tendency towards increasing.

Existential labour is practiced by practically two thirds of humanity, with a tendency towards decreasing.

Ritual labour is practices by the whole of humanity. With very rare individual exceptions.

This shows that ritual labour is incorporated into both existential and creative labour, i.e., that while practicing existential and creative labour man also practices ritual labour. Thus, those who produce necessities for existence, knowledge and health and those who discover unknown canons and processes in nature, at the same time also practice ritual labour dedicated to God, nation, power, glory or material fortune.

This involvement of a vast number of people speaks on its own; ritual labour has an exceptional, I would say vital, role in man's existence and we know that role. We'll repeat it, viewing some qualitative characteristics in these three forms of labour:

Without creative labour humanity would stay at the level of insects.

Without existential labour humanity wouldn't exist, and arguments aren't needed to prove this.

Without ritual labour humanity wouldn't even exist, we have actually assured ourselves of that, namely:

The conscious supremacy of man over man, we experience it subconsciously as the supremacy of eternity over death in whatever would be, and without this subconscious contact with eternity, man is not in a state to live. This is confirmed by the insane pursuit of the supremacy of man over man in all spheres of public life. His majesty supremacy is decorated by the mass media with admiration, gaiety, happiness. Since the humanity knows that, the supremacy of man over man and the collective supremacy of the group of man over another is the most important concern. And this is so because that conscious supremacy offers it eternity, although the fictitious one.

Aggression is a consequence of a tendency to conscious supremacy of man over man, and this conscious supremacy develops into an unconscious supremacy of eternity over death; and that means: AGGRESSION IS PRACTISED ON THE LEVEL OF ETERNITY.

Now let's ask: when aggression occurs on the level of eternity, CAN WE ABOLISH IT WITH A LOWER VALUE THAN ETERNITY? The answer is categorical: we can't. This means, that WE MUST BUILD PEACEFULNESS ON THE LEVEL OF ETERNITY: either on the level of fictitious eternity, only keeping passive aggression, or on the level of real eternity, abolishing all aggressive impulses. Only conscious beings will be able to do the latter. If we practice rituals dedicated to existential labour, creative labour and sex, we'll have peaceful humanity with passive aggression, which will contain the latent danger of developing into active aggression; and if the fate of humanity falls into the hands of conscious beings, than we'll have humanity with passive and active aggression abolished. Of course, for this a Constitution, relevant for every individual member of humanity and humanity as a whole, is needed. I call this Constitution: THE CONSTITUTION OF CONSCIOUSNESS.

THE CONSTITUTION
OF CONSCIOUSNESS

The Constitution only has one statute, and the following articles come from it and don't contradict it.

STATUTE OF CONSCIOUSNESS

EVERY INDIVIDUAL ENSURES ITS OWN EXISTENCE BY TAKING PART IN EXISTENTIAL LABOUR OR IN SOME OF ITS SERVICE ORGANIZATIONS.

Service organizations are:

TRANSPORT of necessities for existence, of raw materials and industrial products and of people.

ENLIGHTENMENT is obligatory for primary and secondary education and for free fertiary education. Only science related to nature and man, as an integral part of nature, are taught.

AN ASSOCIATION OF LINGUISTS, who will work upon making a world language, using the richest languages, with a tendency to express mathematical language in words.

MEDICINE will put aside its study of the causes of infections and other natural deseases, and will cure.

THE JUDICATURE will start with a medical point of view. When every individual has solid conditions for existence, the criminal will be treated as suffering from madness. The pursuit of criminal will be done by the security organs. The investigation will be done by lawyers and doctors. The collective where the offender is working will give the verdict, or if he is unemployed. This will be done by the neighbours.

INFORMATION. Daily events in nature and humanity will be presented by radio and TV from one world centre.

SCIENTIFIC INSTITUTIONS. Here people will work upon scientific problems which occur in the service organizations and in existential labour, and will try to solve the theoretical problems which come from the micro and macro world.

THE PARLIAMENT OF HUMANITY will coordinate relations between existential labour and its serice organizations and will bring recommendations for decreasing the population, because the requirements for life are limited.

ARTICLE 1. The interests of the individual cannot be in contradiction with the interests of humanity and ice versa; as much as the individual gives humanity, that much humanity gives the individual, in harmony with moral standards.

ARTICLE 2. Professionalism in art, philosophy, circus, begging and sports, is not included in the Constitution. The working day will be reduced so much that free time will be filled with art, philosophy, sport and other activities. They'll have their own clubs, and the clubs will have their own palaces of poetry, music, painting, art; palaces of philosophy and sport, where they will display the scope of their creations. For these activities people won't be rewarded in any material form whatever, and no one will be able to ensure his own existence as an artist, philosopher or sportsman. This also applies to the clergy, nationalists and ideologists. They will affirm and praise their own religions, nations or ideologies entirely freely, but without any kind of material reward, and no one will be able to secure his own existence as a cleric, nationalists or ideologists.

This is a short sketch of the Constitution of consciousness.

The first to revolt against the Constitution of consciousness would be the ritualists (i.e. the official representatives) of the states, and usually of the technologically most developed ones. But they are literally threatening humanity with extermination. Where is the danger? Right here: there are organic reflexes for which knowledge and consciousness mean nothing; but there are also "psychological reflexes" for which knowledge, consciousness, all-human moral and scientific knowledge mean nothing. So if, for instance, the communist world* is squeezed territorially to a critical point, "the psychological reflex" will determine nuclear war. In the same situation the capitalist world would do the same thing. We are living in a time in which both worlds are grabbing bits of continents and oceans, for one world to gain supremacy over the other, and, further, to crush it. Consciousness thinks like so, but the unconscious will crush humanity.

---

*This essay was written in time of the cold war

53

Let's ask now: is it better for humanity to accept this Constitution of consciousness or to destroy itself?!?!?!

The Constitution of consciousness can't be realized "over night", nor can it be imposed on people with force by any organized ideology.

"There is no beauty with power", say minority people in the Balkans. The realization of this Constitution will become possible when two thirds of humanity are ashamed of the fact that someone else is ensuing their existence.

The prime question today is: how can active aggression be abolished, and first above all, how to abolish war in general, because even local wars can cause world war? Prevention of war is imperative while the universal fear can paradoxically develop in contradiction to itself.

What is the prime obstacle to the abolishment of war? At this historical moment it is the disparate political ideologies: for the first, private property is "the sacred right" of every citizen, and for the other, public property is "the sacred right" of the citizens. Humanity could destroy itself, just because of these 'scared rights". These "sacred rights" are actually imposed "rights": where social ownership is practiced, there are people who desire private property and where private ownership is practiced, there are people who desire social property, and if the present statement wish to get involved in history, (history is building, not destroying), it's necessary for them to give all INDIVIDUAL MEMBERS OF HUMANITY THE RIGHT TO DETERMINE MOST DEMOCRATICALLY AND MOST FREELY THEIR RELATION TO BOTH PRIVATE, AND, PUBLIC PROPERTY over several decades. Afterwards, the proprietors must take responsibility for the fate of humanity and the fate of every human individual, and in addition, neither social nor the private proprietors must use army freely for exerting physical and psychological pressure.

Both private and social proprietors give great sums of money to their states, which supposedly protect, both private and public property. The states are symbols of two contradictory property relations, and the supremacy of one over the other makes the self-destruction of humanity very real.

It's obvious that HUMANITY OUGHT TO FREE ITSELF, NOT FROM PRIVATE AND PUBLIC PROPERTY, BUT FROM ITS SYMBOLS.

This assumes that present official representatives of states with private and public property will develop into a parliament of humanity, which would decide:

1. All armies of the world must be dismissed, and the arms industry must turn into peace-time industry;

2. No one has the right, from any perspective, to exert influence on individuals in deciding between private and public property;

3. The members of this parliament will be replaced by great scientists, by dint of natural processes. This parliament, stating from a scientific perspective, will take care of the universal well being of humanity on the basis of private and public property. It will have no right to influence the individual's partiality for either private or social property; this partiality, moreover, will be allowed according to the natural impulses of every individual. And so on until conscious beings start to rule.

Without concessions from capitalism and communism a nuclear world war can't be prevented, and concessions are justified by the fact that: ON EARTH THERE ARE NEITHER GUILTY NOR GUILTLESS, THERE ARE HARMFUL AND USEFUL, as in the private, as also in the social sector.

ABOUT THE AUTHOR

The Macedonian author Stefan Tanevski gave the world of drama writing three incredible works "Ivac", "Vladimir and Kosara" and "Rog", all historical ones. The most amazing in those pieces is that all of them are written in verses in, so to say, Shakespearean style. The man who began to show his talent at the age of fifteen by writing poetry, but as a deep philosophical personality, he used to think on life, on God, on nature for all of his life. And all of his works are permeated with those thoughts. The man who has been honored as the Distinguished Member of the International Society of Poets in 1995 for his incredible achievements in poetry.

By his work he wanted to show the world that there's hope for life, that we should live in goodness, in love between ourselves. The misfortune of living in communism stopped him of showing what he wanted to give to this world. And now, the time has come for his ideas, for his thoughts to see the light of day. Though not within the living ones, I'm sure that he looks from above and rejoice himself that his task has been fulfilled with his book been published.